Book bri

1 *The Boat Race Mystery* is an exciting story about the Oxford rowers who are training for the famous Oxford and Cambridge Boat Race.

2 Lots of strange things start to happen to the Oxford squad and Shorty has to leave the team.

3 Shorty's brother, Sam, and his friends must find out who's trying to sabotage the Oxford crew.

4 The story is full of suspense as the reader tries to solve the mystery with Sam and his friends.

5 The story also gives the reader an idea of how hard the rowers have to train for this historic race.

www.eligradedreaders.com

In this reader:

21st Century Skills	To encourage students to connect the story to the world they live in.
MOVERS	A1 level activities.
Story Notes	A brief summary of the text.
Glossary	Explanation of difficult words.
Picture Caption	A brief explanation of the picture.
Audio	These icons indicate the parts of the story that are recorded. start stop
Think	To encourage students to develop their critical thinking skills.

The FSC® certification guarantees that the paper used in these publications comes from certified forests, promoting responsible forestry management worldwide.

FSC www.fsc.org MIX Paper from responsible sources FSC® C127663

For this series of ELI graded readers, we have planted 5000 new trees.

Janet Borsbey & Ruth Swan

The Boat Race Mystery

Illustrated by
Thomas Campi

Teen ELi Readers

Teen Eli Readers

The **ELI Readers** collection is a complete range of books and plays for readers of all ages, ranging from captivating contemporary stories to timeless classics. There are four series, each catering for a different age group: **First ELI Readers, Young ELI Readers, Teen ELI Readers** and **Young Adult ELI Readers**. The books are carefully edited and beautifully illustrated to capture the essence of the stories and plots. The readers are supplemented with 'Focus on' texts packed with background cultural information about the writers and their lives and times.

The Boat Race Mystery
By Janet Borsbey and Ruth Swan
The authors would like to thank:
all the team at Eli and E. Chuther.
A special thanks to Michael Swan and Sidney Theskwid.
Language Level Consultant
Silvana Sardi
Illustrated by **Thomas Campi**
Activities and focus pages by
Janet Borsbey and Ruth Swan

ELI Readers
Founder and Series Editors
Paola Accattoli, Grazia Ancillani, Daniele Garbuglia (Art Director)

Graphic Design
Andersen
the Premedia Company

Production Manager
Francesco Capitano

Photo credits
Shutterstock, Getty Images

New edition: **2021**
First edition: **2014**

P.O. Box 6
62019 Recanati (MC)
Italy
T +39 071750701
F +39 071977851
info@elionline.com
www.elionline.com

Typeset in 12 / 17 pt
Fulmar designed by Leo Philp

Printed in Italy by
Tecnostampa - Pigini Group Printing Division
Loreto - Trevi (Italia) -
ERT 116.10
ISBN 978-88-536-3186-2

Contents

Main Characters

Sam

Shorty's younger brother. With his friends he tries to understand why so many strange things are happening to the Oxford rowing squad.

Shorty

Shorty is very sad when he has to leave the Oxford rowing squad.

The Coach

He must choose the best crew for the Boat Race.

Pete

He's Shorty's best friend and wants to row in the Boat Race for Oxford.

Max

He really wants a place in the Oxford crew for the Boat Race.

Jason

He's very clever and has some great ideas to help his sister, Lisa, and Sam.

Lisa

She tries to help Sam discover who's trying to sabotage the Oxford crew.

Mr. Pullen

He's a nice man who works at the boathouse.

Before you read

Reading and Writing MOVERS

1 **These words are all in the story. Look at the pictures and choose the correct word for each definition.**

train

row

race

jump

win

boathouse

crew

~~squad~~

A large number of people who are working to be in a team. *squad*

1 Use a piece of wood to make a boat go fast. ________
2 The people who are in a water sports team. ________
3 Work very hard to be good at a sport. ________
4 A way to find the best person or team in a sport. ________
5 Be the best in a game or sport. ________

Speaking

21st Century Skills

2 **This story is about the Oxford-Cambridge Boat Race. Work with a partner and go online to answer the questions.**

1 Where's Oxford?
2 Where's Cambridge?
3 How often is the Oxford-Cambridge Boat Race?
4 Do you like water sports? Why? / Why not?
5 What other water sports can you think of?

Vocabulary

3 Put the adjectives into the right sentences. Use your dictionary to help you.

afraid ~~angry~~ lucky proud sure ill

Teachers sometimes shout when they're *angry* .

1 Some people are ________ of flying.
2 In some countries it's ________ to see a black cat.
3 When you have a cold, you feel ________ .
4 'I can't find my pen! I'm ________ I put it on the table.'
5 You feel ________ when you do something well.

Reading and Vocabulary

4 Read this information about rowing in Oxford. Use your English-English dictionary to help you, then write the translation in your language of the words in red.

This book is about three young people who live in Oxford, an old university city in the UK. Oxford is famous for its beautiful university **colleges** and is on the River Thames. There are two exciting college boat races in Oxford every year: Torpids and Eights. The boats start at the same time, about 28 m apart. Each boat has to overtake the boat **in front of** it. The river isn't straight and sometimes the boats have to **turn** to go **around** a **corner**. People stand on the **paths** by the river and on the **bridges** over the river to watch their college boats.

1 a college ________
2 in front of ________
3 to turn ________
4 a corner ________
5 around ________
6 a path ________
7 a bridge ________

Chapter 1

Shorty Comes Home

The coach says Shorty must leave the squad. Shorty says he didn't do anything. His best friend Pete doesn't say or do anything to help him.

2 'I didn't do it! I didn't do it, Coach[1]!'

'I'm sorry, Shorty,' said the coach in a quiet voice[2], 'but I can't help you. I don't want you in the squad any more.'

The coach opened the door and left the Oxford boathouse. Shorty, the tallest person in the squad, looked at the other rowers. No one said anything.

'I didn't do anything,' said Shorty. He looked at his best friend. 'Pete?'

Pete didn't look up.

'You heard the coach, Shorty, now go,' someone said.

'You're not the coach, Max,' said one of the Australians. 'Come with me, Shorty, come outside.'

The two young men left the room. Someone laughed[3]. Shorty was sure it was Max.

Back inside the boathouse, three of the rowers were angry. 'Why didn't you say anything, Pete?' asked one of the Canadians. 'He's your best friend! Why didn't you go with him?'

[1] **coach** someone who teaches people to play a sport better
[2] **voice** you use your voice when you speak. Your voice makes the noise
[3] **laugh** when you think something is funny, you often laugh. You make a noise because you're happy

Pete didn't answer; he looked at his feet.

Max, of course, had a lot to say. 'Pete's afraid! He wants to stay in the squad. Coach is right; Shorty's the problem. We can't row with someone like[1] him.'

• • •

It was a long bike ride from the river to Shorty's parents' house past all the colleges. Shorty didn't know what to do. He didn't know how to tell his parents. They were very proud of him. They were proud of him because he was a student at the famous university; and they were proud of him because he had a place in the Oxford rowing squad. He rode slowly, thinking about his parents and then he remembered Sam. Sam! Shorty went around the corner into his street and there he was, his brother Sam, in the garden, playing baseball with that funny girl.

Shorty doesn't know how to tell his parents that he isn't in the Oxford rowing squad anymore. He's worried and angry. He doesn't even want to speak to his brother.

'Shorty!' shouted[2] Sam. 'How was training? How's my famous brother?'

'Shut up[3],' said Shorty, getting off[4] his bike. 'Are Mum and Dad home?'

'Dad's in the garden, Mum's at work.'

[1] **like** the same as
[2] **shout** when someone can't hear you, you make a lot of noise when you speak
[3] **shut up** be quiet, don't speak
[4] **get off** when you get off your bike, you stop riding it. You walk or run

Sam tells Lisa to shut up because she says something bad about his brother, Shorty. His brother and father are talking in the garden. Then his mum comes home and Sam sees that Shorty is crying.

Shorty walked past his brother and into the house. Sam and Lisa looked at each other.

'What's wrong with him?' said Lisa. 'Is he too important to speak to his little brother?'

'Shut up!' shouted Sam, and he ran into the house.

From the kitchen window, Sam could see his brother and his father in the back garden, but he couldn't hear them. He decided[1] not to go outside. He watched for a long time. Then, he heard the door open and his mother walked into the kitchen. 'Hello, Sam,' she said. 'Good day at school? Where's your father?'

'In the garden. He's talking to Shorty.'

'Your brother's home early,' said Sam's mum.

'I know and he isn't very happy.'

'What's wrong, Sam?' Sam's mum was afraid.

Everyone thinks Shorty took money from the boathouse because it was in his bag. That's why he isn't in the squad anymore, but he says he didn't do it.

Then, Shorty looked up. He saw his mum and brother at the kitchen window.

'Shorty's crying[2] like a baby!' said Sam. 'Why's he crying?'

A short time later, they understood why.

'Someone took some money from the boathouse,' said Shorty. 'Everyone thinks it was me. The money was in my bag, but I didn't take it; someone put it there. It wasn't me.'

›

The coach is angry with Shorty. He thinks he took some money from the boathouse because they found it in Shorty's bag. He says Shorty can't stay in the squad.

[1] **decide** when you think about doing something then you do it
[2] **cry** people cry when they're sad and babies cry when they're hungry

OXFOR

'But why did someone do that?' asked his father.

'I don't know. But I'm not in the squad any more and everyone thinks I took the money.'

'Of course you didn't!' said Sam. 'There's an answer to this. Don't worry.'

• • •

Sam can't sleep because he's worried about his brother. He's sure Shorty didn't take the money but he needs to know who put the money in his brother's bag.

Sam couldn't sleep that night. *What's the problem at the boathouse? Why did someone put the money in Shorty's bag?* he thought. *Why does everyone think it was my brother? Shorty doesn't cry.*

At about four o'clock in the morning, he turned on the light[1]. *I need to make a plan*[2], he thought. *It's Saturday tomorrow. I need to talk to Lisa. We need to know who took the money and who put it in Shorty's bag.*

Sam meets Lisa the next morning and tells her everything. They decide to start at the boathouse.

The next morning, Sam had breakfast very early. He put on his jacket and got his baseball things. 'We've got a game, see you later,' he said to his father as he ran outside.

It was half-past eight when Sam arrived[3] at Lisa's house. It was very quiet. He decided to send a message.

Meet me outside now with your baseball things.

Five minutes later, Lisa came outside.

[1] **light** when a room is dark you need a light to see
[2] **make a plan** a plan helps you to know what to do
[3] **arrive** you arrive at school in the morning and you leave school in the afternoon

'I'm sorry that I shouted at you, yesterday,' said Sam in a quiet voice.

'That's OK. What's wrong?' she asked. 'Is it Shorty?'

Sam told Lisa everything.

'We must start at the boathouse,' she said. 'The answer is at the boathouse.'

'LISA JANE HARTLEY! Come back here!' they heard from Lisa's house. 'Take Jason with you this morning.'

'MUM! I'm playing baseball this morning. He's too young!' Then she said to Sam, 'Aren't we lucky? We're fourteen and he's eleven!'

'Don't worry, your brother's OK,' said Sam. 'Perhaps[1] he can help.'

Jason ran outside. 'Where are we going?' he asked. He was very happy.

'To the river,' said Sam.

'Boring,' said Jason.

• • •

Down at the river, it was very quiet. It was warm for late October. The three friends decided to sit on a wall by the boathouse and make a plan.

'We need to know about the money. We need to talk to everyone,' said Lisa.

'Shh. They're coming,' said Sam.

A group of rowers arrived at the boathouse by

Sam and Lisa have to take Lisa's brother Jason with them. They go to the boathouse and a group of rowers arrive. They hear them talking.

[1] **perhaps** you say 'perhaps' when you aren't sure about something

bike. 'Today's the day!' said one of them.

'Don't!' said one of the others.

'What does he mean?' asked Lisa.

The coach has to decide the crew for the boat race. Lisa thinks this is perhaps a motive for what happened to Shorty.

'The coach must decide the crew for the boat race today. Well, the final eight and two others. Everyone else goes into the second boat.'

'Mmm,' said Lisa. 'That's a motive.'

'What does motive mean?' asked Jason.

'It's why you do something. The police always look for a motive. Shh.'

Some more rowers came around the corner, got off their bikes and left them outside the boathouse. They went inside. Then, more rowers arrived with the coach, but no one looked at the three friends on the wall.

The three friends see Mr Pullen. He says he's sure Shorty didn't take the money.

Sam, Lisa and Jason waited outside. Jason was bored, and he got off the wall and he started to play with the ball.

An old man in work clothes came outside from a small door in the boathouse. 'Hello, Sam,' he said.

'Hello, Mr Pullen,' said Sam.

'I'm sorry about Shorty,' said Mr Pullen. 'He didn't take that money, I'm sure. And he's a very good rower.'

'Pullen!' Someone shouted from the boathouse. 'Come and help me with this seat!'

'Coming Max,' said Mr Pullen and he walked into the boathouse.

Sam, Lisa and Jason are waiting outside the boathouse. Mr Pullen speaks to them. He's sure Shorty didn't take the money.

Think

What do you think Sam and Lisa can do to help Shorty?

Mets

Reading Comprehension

1 Characters. Complete the sentences with the name and the possessive 's.

Lisa is *Mrs Hartley's* daughter.
1 Lisa is ________________ friend.
2 Jason is ________________ brother.
3 Jason is ________________ son.
4 Shorty is ________________ brother.
5 Pete is ________________ best friend.

Writing

2A Lisa didn't want her mum to understand her message to Sam. Use the key below. Can you read her message?

EQF NGX EGDT ZG ZIT KOCTK ZGDGKKGV?
WKOFU NGXK WQLTWQSS ZIOFUL.

_ _?

_ _.

Q=A	W=B	E=C	R=D	T=E	Y=F	U=G	I=H
O=I	P=J	A=K	S=L	D=M	F=N	G=O	H=P
J=Q	K=R	L=S	Z=T	X=U	C=V	V=W	B=X
N=Y	M=Z						

21st Century Skills

2B Can you see how the code works? The message below will help.

SGGA QZ ZIT STZZTKL GF Q ATNWGQKR.

_ _.

2C Work in pairs. Use the key. Write your own message for your partner.

Vocabulary

3 When there is too much rain, people can't row. Look at the Oxford rain chart. Write the months in the sentences.

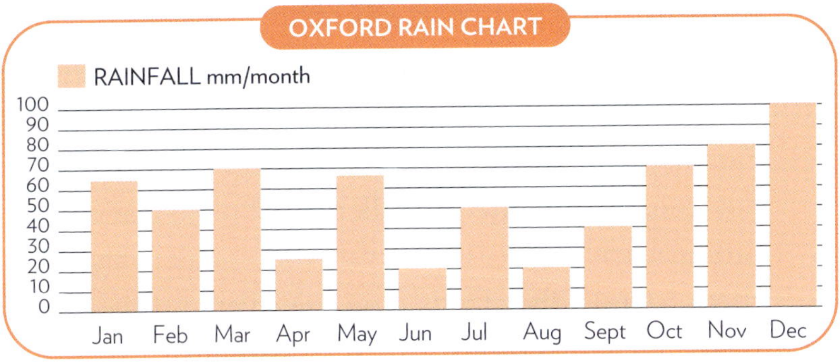

There was 20 mm more rain in *September* than in August.

1 ____________ and ____________ were the driest months.

2 ____________ was the wettest month.

3 There was 20 mm less rain in ____________ than in December.

4 In ____________ and ____________ there was 10 mm less rain than in November.

5 There was the same amount of rain in January and ____________ .

Before-reading Activity

Reading and Writing MOVERS

4 Look at the picture on page 27. Complete the sentences and answer the questions.

The boathouse is on *fire* .

1 Who's looking at the fire? ____________

2 Lisa has got long blond ____________ .

3 What time of day is it? ____________

4 What's Jason wearing? ____________

Chapter 2

Fire[1]!

3 Sam, Lisa and Jason went to the river the next day, too. They wanted to talk to Mr Pullen again, but he wasn't there. The rowers didn't talk to the three friends; they trained on the river and then talked for a long time inside the boathouse.

Sam, Lisa and Jason go to the river again, but they can't hear what the rowers say in the boathouse. They don't know who's in the crew and why somebody didn't want Shorty.

'We need to hear what they're saying,' said Lisa.

'Yes,' said Sam, 'we don't know anything. We aren't sure who's in the crew. Someone didn't want Shorty in the crew, but I don't know why.'

'Perhaps Shorty's too good,' said Jason.

Lisa laughed at her brother. 'No! Why? They all want Oxford to win!'

Sam thought for a minute. 'Perhaps Jason's right,' he said. 'Shorty's not in the crew, now there's a place for one more rower.'

Lisa laughed again. 'Perhaps the coach is from *Cambridge*! But we need a better plan. We can't watch them every day.'

The next Saturday, the three friends were down at the river again, and the rowers were on the river in front of them. Mr Pullen was there, working on one of the boats.

[1] **fire** see page 27 - the boathouse is on fire

'We've got a question,' said Lisa. 'Why did someone put the money in Shorty's bag?'

Mr Pullen stopped work. 'I'm not sure. Everyone wants a place in the final crew, but something's wrong. I'm sure someone was in the boathouse late last night; the door wasn't closed this morning.'

'Did the person take any more money from the boathouse?'

'No. Now, come on, play your baseball. I've got a lot of work to finish.' He wasn't angry, but Mr Pullen didn't want to talk any more.

Sam, Lisa and Jason went to sit on the wall. Sam and Lisa threw the ball to each other. Jason watched.

'Why is someone coming to the boathouse at night? Is the person looking for something?' said Sam.

'Perhaps we can come back tonight and watch,' said Jason.

'I can't tonight,' said Sam.

'Well tomorrow, then.'

'Mum's birthday,' said Lisa.

'Monday!' said Jason. He wanted to watch the boathouse at night very much.

'It's a school night!' said Sam.

The three friends made a plan and then stayed

Mr Pullen doesn't know who put the money in Shorty's bag but he says that everyone wants a place in the final crew. He's sure someone was in the boathouse the night before. Sam, Lisa and Jason would like to watch the boathouse at night, but they can't decide which night.

Sam, Lisa and Jason make a plan and stay to watch the team. They see that Pete, Shorty's best friend, and Max aren't in the crew.

at the river all morning. They wanted to know who was in the crew. But it was sad to watch the squad without Shorty.

'That's Pete Arnold, Shorty's best friend,' said Sam, getting off the wall and pointing[1] at a smaller boat. 'And that rower is Max. Look, they aren't in the crew. Pete and Max aren't in the crew!'

• • •

Monday morning was grey and cold. Sam waited for Lisa outside school to talk about their plan.

'Mum says OK for tonight. I can come and study at your house after school,' she said.

Lisa's mum thinks that Lisa wants to study at Sam's and Sam's mum thinks that Sam wants to study at Lisa's. This is part of their plan so they can go to the boathouse at night. Jason has got a guitar lesson.

'And my mum says I can come to your house to study. It's lucky that my mum doesn't know your mum! What about Jason?'

'Mum says no; he's got a guitar lesson.'

It was a long, slow morning at school. The grey weather didn't help and two maths lessons before lunch were always yuck! Sam didn't see Lisa at lunchtime. The afternoon was slow too. Then, the last lesson ended and Sam and Lisa ran outside. It was only four o'clock, but it was dark. Sam didn't like winter mornings or winter evenings. They walked quickly down the road and then turned

›

The boys in the crew are training for the Boat Race. They're rowing on the river.

[1] **point**  the finger in this picture is pointing

the corner into a smaller road. They didn't talk, they walked quietly. There weren't as many street lights on this road and now it was dark. They were both a little afraid. Then, they heard a noise in a garden. Lisa took Sam's arm and something jumped in front of them! 'Aargh!' they shouted.

There, in front of them, was Jason, with his guitar.

Lisa shouted, 'Jason! Don't do that again, you ...!'

'Shh!' said Sam. 'People mustn't hear us. Jason! Don't jump out like that. Lisa was afraid, and so was I. Now, come on, we need to go to the river.'

'What about your lesson?' said Lisa as they walked.

'I phoned,' said Jason.

• • •

Jason doesn't go to his guitar lesson. Sam and Lisa are afraid when he jumps out in front of them. They all go to the river. It's dark at the boathouse and they sit and wait. Then they hear something.

The boathouse was dark and quiet. There were no boats on the river. They could see the lights from some houses, but they were in the distance[1]. They couldn't hear anything: there were no cars, no buses, no people. The three friends sat quietly on the wall and waited. They waited and waited. 'What was that?' Sam said.

'I didn't hear anything', said Jason, 'and I'm hungry.'

They all heard it; the noise of bike wheels[2] on the path. The three friends were behind the wall

[1] **in the distance** not near you
[2] **a wheel** a bike has got 2 wheels. A car has got 4 wheels

and, of course, they couldn't see anything. They heard the person get off the bike, then nothing. About ten minutes later, they heard the bike wheels again. 'He's leaving!' said Lisa.

Jason and Sam got up. They could see the red of the bike's back light in the distance.

'Oh no!' shouted Lisa, afraid. 'Look! Fire!'

There was a light at the back of the boathouse. The three friends ran around the corner to look. They could see smoke inside the boathouse. Lisa was very fast. 'Run,' she shouted. 'We need help!' And she phoned 999[1] on her mobile.

She listened for a minute, then said, 'Fire! There's a fire at the river. It's the Oxford Boathouse!'

Sam, Lisa and Jason waited by the wall. The fire was bigger now. Then, in the distance, they heard the noise of a fire engine[2]. The firefighters[3] were very quick. After about ten minutes, one of them came to talk to the three friends. 'It's lucky you saw the fire,' he said, 'but I think the police want to talk to you.'

'Hello there,' a police officer said to Lisa, in a

Someone arrives on a bike but the three friends can't see who it is because they're behind a wall. The person stays at the boathouse for ten minutes then goes away. Suddenly Lisa sees the boathouse is on fire and phones 999.

The firefighters are quick. It was lucky that the three friends saw the fire. The police want to talk to Sam, Lisa and Jason.

[1] **999** the official emergency phone number in the UK to contact the police, fire service and ambulance service

[2] **fire engine** see page 27. One of the men is standing on this to get near the fire

[3] **firefighter** see page 27. There are two firefighters here trying to stop the fire

nice voice, 'are you the girl who called 999?'

'Yes, I'm Lisa Jane Hartley.'

'Thank you,' the police officer made a note, 'and why were you here at the boathouse?'

The three friends tell the police they were near the boathouse because Jason has his guitar lesson near there and that they saw a tall man on a bike. Now there's a problem ... what if the police officer speaks to their mums?

'My brother, Jason: he has a music lesson there,' Lisa pointed at the colleges and houses in the distance.

Jason showed the police officer his guitar.

'Yes,' said Sam, 'it's lucky. We were near the boathouse when we saw a man on a bike. He came from near the boathouse. He followed[1] the path, there.' Sam pointed at the path. 'Then we saw the fire and Lisa called 999.'

'What did he look like? Young or old? Tall or short?'

'Tall,' said Sam, 'but it was dark.'

'Well, thank you,' said the police officer, 'I'd like your addresses, please. Then you can take your brother to his music lesson.'

On their way home, the friends talked and talked. 'Jason,' said Sam, 'phew! I'm happy that you've got your guitar! And, Lisa, you were very quick to call!'

'Yes, but we've got a problem, Sam,' said Lisa. '*Our* mum and *your* mum! What can we say? What if the police come to visit?'

Think

What do you think Sam and Lisa can say to their mums if the police officer comes to ask them more questions at home?

›

The three friends watch the firefighters trying to put out the fire in the boathouse.

[1] **follow** (here) use the path. Follow also means to go behind someone and to go to the same places

Reading Comprehension

1 Who am I? Read the description and say which character it is.

1 I've got a brother. I'm tall. I'm sad at the moment.
What's my name? ____________________
2 I've got a brother. I've got a friend called Sam. I called 999.
What's my name? ____________________
3 I'm an old man. I like Sam, Lisa and Jason. I work at the boathouse.
What's my name? ____________________
4 I haven't got a brother. I'm younger than Sam. I play the guitar.
What's my name? ____________________
5 I've got a brother. I go to school with Lisa. I love baseball.
What's my name? ____________________

Test your Skills

21st Century Skills

2 Can you help Jason with his maths homework?

It's Saturday on the River Thames. This is what you can see:

1 There are 2 x 5 boats. How many boats are there? __________
2 People watching x 2 = rowers training. How many rowers are training? __________
3 Ducks – 8 = people watching. How many people are watching? __________
4 People watching ÷ 2 = bridges over the river. How many bridges are there over the river? __________
5 Boats + 8 = ducks. How many ducks are there? __________
6 How many people and things are there in total? __________

Reading and Writing MOVERS

3 Look at this picture from Chapter 2. Complete the sentences and answer the questions.

The rowers are in the *boat*.

1 Two rowers are wearing ______.

2 What can you see behind them? ______

3 How many men are rowing? ______

4 Where are they rowing? ______

Before-reading Activity

Listening

▶ 4 **4 Work in pairs and answer the questions about Chapter 3. Say why you think these things happen. Then, listen to the first part of Chapter 3 and circle yes or no.**

1 Is Lisa's mum proud? yes/no

2 Does Sam tell his mum and dad about the fire? yes/no

3 Does Sam go down to the river the next weekend? yes/no

4 Was it sunny the next Saturday? yes/no

5 Was Sam bored on Sunday? yes/no

Chapter 3

Get an Ambulance!

4 Lisa and Jason's mum was angry. She was angry with Jason about the music lesson, but she was angrier with Lisa. 'You can stay at home for the next three weekends helping me!' she shouted.

Lisa's mum is very angry with her and says she must stay at home. Sam's parents are angry when they hear about the boathouse fire but they're more afraid about Shorty.

Sam told his parents about the boathouse fire, too. They were angry with him, but they were more afraid about Shorty.

Sam went down to the river the next weekend, but the rowers weren't there. It was difficult, because Lisa and Jason weren't there. Then, it was a very slow week at school and when Saturday came, it rained and rained. Sunday was the same. Shorty was out and Sam was bored. He finished his homework. He played a computer game and listened to some music and it was only 3 o'clock. He wanted to talk to Mr Pullen, but he couldn't.

5 The next Saturday, the weather was fine for November. Sam arrived at the river very early. No one was there. He sat on the wall. His hands were cold.

'Is it only you today?' asked Mr Pullen, getting off his bike. 'It was lucky that you three saw the fire.'

'Yes,' said Sam. 'Were the boats OK after the fire?'

'Oh, yes. There was no problem.' Mr Pullen walked up to the boathouse door.

'One thing, Mr Pullen.'

'Yes, Sam?'

'We saw a tall man. He started the fire. We told the police.'

'I know,' said Mr Pullen. 'Are you coming to the December Race next Saturday? Max and Pete are training very hard; they both want a place in the crew. I'm sorry Shorty isn't training with them.'

Sam phoned Lisa when he got home, but Mrs Hartley answered the phone. 'She's working in the garden. She can't speak to you now,' she said.

Sam decided to send Lisa a message.

Talked to Mr Pullen. December Race next Saturday. Can you come?

It was four o'clock when Lisa phoned. She was excited. 'The December Race! What's that?'

'Lisa! Put that phone DOWN and COME HERE!' Sam heard.

Sam speaks to Mr Pullen. The December Race is next Saturday. He tries to talk to Lisa about it but her mum tells her to put the phone down.

'It's Mum,' said Lisa to Sam. 'One more job for me. I have to go.' She wanted to cry.

At school on Monday, Lisa spoke to Sam. 'Well, what's the December Race?' she said.

'The coach decides the final crew: Max and Pete want a place in the crew.'

Sam tells Lisa that the December Race is important because the coach decides the final crew. Pete and Max want a place in the final crew so they're training hard. Jason has a plan. He wants to listen to the people and the noises in the boathouse.

'We have to go. One more thing – Jason wants to listen to the people and the noises in the boathouse. He's got a plan; he's working on it.'

'I told you. Be proud of your brother. He's clever!'

• • •

Saturday came and Sam went down to the river, early, with Lisa and Jason. They walked down the path for a long time: they wanted to see the end of the first race. They waited and then they heard the race start. A minute or two later, they heard people shouting, but where were the boats?

'What's the problem? Where are they?' shouted Sam.

'I don't know, why aren't they here?'

'The bridge!' shouted Jason.

The three friends ran. They ran up the path from the river to Donnington Bridge. There were some people on the bridge watching the river.

'Who's winning? Who's winning?' Sam asked one of them.

'Not sure,' said a student. 'They aren't rowing.'

'It looks like an accident[1],' said Jason. 'I can see one of the rowers. I think he's hurt[2].'

Then everyone on the bridge turned and looked at the road. In the distance, they could see the blue lights of an ambulance.

The three friends go to see the December Race, but there's something wrong. A rower is hurt and an ambulance arrives.

• • •

At the boathouse, everyone was very quiet. It was difficult to see, because there were a lot of people around one of the boats. It was lucky that Sam was tall.

'What can you see?' said Jason.

'One of the rowers is hurt. I can't see who. No, it's one of the Australians. They're taking him to the ambulance now. It's his arm. The coach is looking at the seat. A wheel! There are only three wheels on the seat!'

'Sabotage[3]!' said Jason.

'Yes,' said Lisa, 'there's a place for Max or Pete in the crew now.'

Sam was quiet.

The ambulance took the rower to hospital and the police arrived; they asked everyone to leave.

One of the Australians has to go to hospital. The coach sees that the seat only has three wheels, so someone planned the accident. Lisa says now there's a place in the crew for Pete or Max. The police arrive.

[1] **accident** when something bad suddenly happens and someone is hurt

[2] **hurt** if something hurts you, you feel bad and sometimes you need to go to hospital

[3] **sabotage** when somebody does something bad to stop a team winning, it's sabotage

The three friends think the accident was sabotage because someone wants the rower's place in the crew.

The three friends walked slowly down the path. They sat on the grass near the bridge for a short time. Sam threw his baseball up and caught it. 'I think Jason's right,' he said. 'It was sabotage. Someone wants that rower's place in the crew.' He threw the ball to Jason, who couldn't catch it. Jason ran to get it, but didn't see a rower riding his bike quickly down the path. The rower stopped. 'Sorry,' said Jason. 'I didn't see you.'

Max shouts at Jason because he runs in front of him to get his ball. Max wants a place in the crew. Lisa doesn't like him.

'Get some new glasses, little boy!' the rower shouted. 'Don't throw your ball here. I don't want to have an accident, I'm in the Oxford squad and I want to win!'

'That was Max!' said Sam.

'Max? He wants a place in the crew,' said Lisa, 'and I don't like him at all.'

On Sunday morning, everything about the hurt rower was in the newspaper.

The story of the accident is in the newspaper. It says that Pete Arnold is in the crew now because the other rower hurt his arm.

ROWING ACCIDENT – OXFORD MAN HURT

Oxford rower, Sid Forster, 22, is in hospital this morning after a wheel on his seat broke in the December Race, yesterday. The police are talking to everyone in the squad. Forster, from Melbourne, Australia, hurt his arm and cannot row in the Oxford-Cambridge Boat Race. His place in the crew goes to Pete Arnold.

There's an accident and one of the rowers hurts his arm. They take him to hospital.

Shorty is happy that Pete is in the crew. Sam says that place is Shorty's.

'I'm happy that Pete's in the crew. His father must be happy, too,' said Shorty. 'Pete can row for Oxford, like his father.'

'It's your place,' said Sam, eating his bread and jam.

'No, it isn't,' Shorty answered, sadly. 'I'm going to the gym.'

Sam went outside too. He went to Lisa's house, but there was no one there. He walked down to the river. There were some boats on the river, but not very many. Sam decided to go home. The sky was dark in the distance. 'More rain!' thought Sam. He turned the corner into Canal Street, and saw it. In front of his house, there was a police car. Then, the door to his house opened and a man came outside. Then Shorty came outside, and a second man followed him. The first man got into the car; he was the driver. Then the second man sat in the back seat of the car with Shorty. Sam couldn't speak. He couldn't cry, he couldn't do anything, and the police left, with his brother.

Sam goes out for a walk. When he comes home, he sees the police taking his brother away.

Think

Why do you think the police came for Shorty?

›

Sam comes home and sees the police taking his brother, Shorty, away.

After-reading Activities • Chapter 3

Vocabulary and Speaking

21st Century Skills

1 A Match the pictures with the sports. Name the sport.

1 There are eleven people on a team and two teams play each other. You need a ball to play. This is one of the most popular sports in the world and you usually play it outside. ____________

2 This isn't a team sport, but sometimes two people play together. You can play inside or outside. You need a ball and a net. Each player has a racket. ____________

3 One, two, four or eight people do this sport on water. Sometimes another person sits in the boat with them. ____________

4 There are nine people on a team and two teams play each other. You need a ball to play this sport and you also need a bat. ____________

5 This is a very popular sport in the USA. There are eleven people on a team. You need a ball to play it, but the ball isn't round. Some players wear a helmet. ____________

6 There are two teams in this sport and you play outside. You need a bat to play. Players often wear white. Matches can be very long. ____________

1 B Work in pairs. Ask and answer these questions.

1 Do you like sport?
2 Do you like watching sport?
3 What's your favourite sport?
4 How often do you play or do it?
5 Which sports don't you like?

Reading and Writing MOVERS

2 Choose the correct word for each sentence about Chapter 3.

Jason's mum was angry with him *about* the music lesson.

~~about~~ to at

1 On Saturday, Sam arrived ________ the river very early.

on at in

2 Max and Pete both want a place ________ the crew.

from by in

3 There were some people ________ the bridge watching the river.

on up down

4 The ambulance took the rower ________ hospital.

at from to

5 The three friends sat ________ the grass near the bridge.

down on in

Before-reading Activity

Speaking

3 A Work in pairs. Here are some things that happen in Chapter 4. Use your imagination to answer the questions.

1 Sam reads something in the newspaper. What does he read?
2 Sam finds out something very good. What is it?
3 Jason is making something. What is it?
4 Sam, Lisa and Jason see someone at the boathouse. Who do they see?
5 The friends talk to Max. What does he say?
6 The coach phones Shorty. What does the coach say?

3 B Now read Chapter 4 and check your answers.

Chapter 4

Talking to Max

6 The next day, at school, Lisa came to find Sam. 'There was something in the newspaper. The police know all about the sabotage. They took someone to the police station yesterday!'

'I know,' said Sam. 'They came for Shorty yesterday.'

The police take Shorty away because they think he has something to do with the sabotage. Then they bring him home. They know it wasn't him because now four of the rowers are ill and he was with the police when this happened.

'*Shorty*?'

'Yes. They're wrong. I know they're wrong.'

'OF COURSE they're wrong!' said Lisa. 'We have to DO something.'

'I'm going to the boathouse after school.'

'I want to come with you and Jason, too!'

After school, it was dark, but Sam, Lisa and Jason ran down to the boathouse. The boathouse was closed, but Mr Pullen was there. 'No training today,' he said. 'Two of the rowers are ill, very ill. We think there was a problem with something they ate or something they drank.'

The next morning was very good. Shorty came home with the same two police officers! 'They know it wasn't me,' he said, 'because now, four of the rowers are ill.'

'Four?' said Sam. 'I thought it was two.'

'Look at this,' said Shorty. He gave Sam the newspaper.

MORE BLUES FOR OXFORD

Two more rowers from the Oxford rowing crew are ill. Now four rowers are ill. Max Harrison and three other rowers from the second crew must take their places for the next two weeks. Police think that this is one more example of sabotage.

The newspaper writes about the sabotage. Max and three others must take the place of the rowers who are ill. The police think it's sabotage again.

'It's Max, I know it's Max!' said Lisa later, at school.

'Yes,' said Sam, 'but think about it. We need to see him doing something bad. We need to go to the boathouse after school every day.'

'Yes. Jason's making a recording thing[1]. He wants to put it in the boathouse; then we can listen to their conversations. I didn't think he was clever, but I was wrong. He's very clever, my little brother.'

It was a little late when Sam and Lisa arrived at the boathouse, and there was no one there. They sat quietly behind the wall and waited. They didn't have to wait long this time. Someone arrived by bike. The person was tall and his clothes were dark: it was Max! Max walked around

Lisa and Sam think Max is the one who's doing all these bad things, but they need to see him doing something bad. Jason wants to record the people speaking in the boathouse. Sam and Lisa see Max arriving at the boathouse.

[1] **a recording thing** (verb = record) his 'recording thing' is a machine he can use to listen later to what people say. He can listen again and again on his computer.

the boathouse and looked into the high windows. He waited for about an hour and then he left.

'Why didn't he do anything?' said Sam.

Sam and Lisa watch Max at the boathouse but he doesn't do anything.

'I don't know. Perhaps he was here to meet someone,' said Lisa. 'I have to go home. I don't want Mum to get angry again.'

• • •

It was the second training race of the day, and the rowers from the Oxford crew were all tired. The January sun was going down when they finished, and the river was beautiful. Some of the rowers took their bikes and went to their colleges. Some stayed to talk, but soon, only Max was left. He looked at the river: he could see the beautiful university colleges in the distance. He walked slowly over the bridge, turned the corner and went home to his college. When he arrived at the college door, he heard a voice. 'Hey, we want to talk to you!'

Lisa, Sam and Jason stop Max at his college. They want to talk to him.

Max turned around quickly. 'Did you follow me from the river?' he asked.

'We want to talk to you,' said Sam again. 'We saw you at the boathouse last night.'

›

The three friends stop Max at the college to talk to him about the sabotage.

The Oxford Times
More blues for Oxford
FESTIVAL

'Oh, did you?' he laughed. 'Well, I'm in the crew, I often go to the boathouse. You're not in the crew, why were you three there?'

'YOU did it!' shouted Lisa.

'Did what?'

'Sabotage!' shouted Sam. 'YOU took the money, YOU started the fire, YOU broke the wheel on the seat and YOU hurt Sid.'

Max says he didn't do anything bad and that he wants to stop the sabotage. The three friends don't know what to do.

Max laughed. 'You're wrong. I don't like your brother, but I know he didn't take the money. I want to know who did. I want to know why so many rowers are ill.'

'Why? Why do you want to help Shorty?'

'I don't want to help him, but I want to stop the sabotage. Now go home!' Max walked into his college.

Sam, Lisa and Jason didn't know what to do.

• • •

The weather in January was very bad. Sam and Lisa worked hard on their homework and Jason worked on his recorder.

'What's that?' said Lisa, laughing when she saw it.

'It's part of a baby listener,' said Jason in an adult voice.

'I remember. It was in your room when you

were a baby. Mum could hear you from the living room when you cried,' said Lisa. 'Well?'

'I'd like a video camera, but we haven't got any money. This is the important part,' Jason pointed at a big black box. 'There's an old recorder in there. We can record conversations, like the police. We need to put the baby listener into the boathouse.'

Jason makes his recorder. Now the only problem is how to put it in the boathouse.

'Good work!' said Lisa. 'We need to tell Sam.'

Sam was very happy, 'We need this. The problems at the boathouse aren't finished. We only have one problem. *How* do we put the recorder *into* the boathouse?

• • •

Two or three days later, the coach phoned Shorty. 'I was wrong, Shorty,' he said. 'Please come back into the squad. I want to choose the new crew next week.'

The coach tells Shorty he's back in the squad. Shorty trains hard and the coach puts him in the crew for Saturday's race.

Shorty was very happy. What did he do? Well, of course, he went to the gym.

Shorty worked hard for the coach. He ran, he rowed and he trained and trained. At the end of the week, the coach came to talk to him. 'You're in the crew for Saturday,' he said.

After training, Pete wanted to talk to Shorty. 'I'm happy that you're back in the crew,' he said.

Pete is happy that Shorty is back in the crew, but nobody knows who's in the final crew for the Boat Race.

'Thanks, Pete,' said Shorty, 'but remember, I'm in the crew for Saturday's race, not for the Boat Race.'

'I know, but no one knows who's in the final crew. *You* don't know, *Max* doesn't know, and *I* don't know.'

• • •

Saturday morning came, and Sam met Lisa and Jason down at the river. The rowers were in the boathouse.

'Look at this,' said Jason. He was very proud of his recorder.

'How does it work?' asked Sam.

Saturday comes and Shorty, Max and Pete are in the race. Sam has a plan to put the recorder in the boathouse.

'Turn this on here, then we can hear everything in the boathouse. There's one problem. We can only record for twenty-four hours.'

'Mmm,' said Sam. 'Twenty-four hours? You are clever. Can I take this?'

'Yes,' said Jason.

'You see,' said Sam, 'I've got a plan. I know how we can put the recorder into the boathouse. I think ...'

He didn't have time to tell Lisa and Jason. The three friends heard the noise of the boathouse door opening. There they were - the Oxford rowers with their boat. They saw Max, they saw Pete and then, they saw Shorty. Sam was very proud of his brother, and excited about his plan. ■

The Oxford rowers are with their boat. There's Max, Pete and Shorty, too. Sam is very proud of his brother.

Think

What do you think of Max?

OXFORD

Reading and Writing MOVERS

1 Choose the correct word for each sentence about Chapter 4.

Mr Pullen *tells* the three friends that two of the rowers are ill.

~~tells~~ says speaks

1 The three friends ________ to go to the boathouse every day.

must need can

2 They can use Jason's recorder to listen ________ the rowers in the boathouse.

at for to

3 The friends haven't got ________ money to buy a video camera.

some any no

4 Jason is very proud ________ his recorder.

of at from

5 With the recorder, they can hear ________ in the boathouse.

some none everything

Vocabulary

2 Wordsearch. Find the opposite of these adjectives in the wordsearch.

new *old*

1 slow ________

2 sad ________

3 easy ________

4 right ________

5 tall ________

6 old ________

7 well ________

L	F	D	S	H	O	R	T
Y	E	I	P	A	U	L	D
O	T	F	S	P	H	D	Y
L	R	F	T	P	D	L	O
D	D	I	A	Y	I	P	U
I	L	C	E	F	R	D	N
L	L	U	R	N	A	E	G
R	F	L	K	V	E	S	W
R	T	T	H	M	E	R	T

Writing and Speaking

3 A **Jason invented a recorder in Chapter 4. Now you want to enter an inventions competition. You can use any type of technology, real or invented! Work in pairs.**

YOUNG INVENTOR OF THE YEAR

Invent a new type of

PEN • CAR • HOME CINEMA • PHONE

Just tell us about your invention!

Name: ______________________

Function: ______________________

Cost: ______________________

Special Features: ______________________

3 B **Tell your class about your invention.**

21st Century Skills

Before-reading Activity

Reading and Listening

4 A **Work in pairs. Before you listen, decide if these sentences are true or false. Use your imagination.**

		T	F
1	The next morning, Sam arrives at the boathouse early.	☐	☐
2	Sam and Mr Pullen have a cup of coffee together.	☐	☐
3	Sam helps Mr Pullen with a boat.	☐	☐
4	Sam puts Jason's recorder into the boathouse.	☐	☐
5	Sam wants to help Mr Pullen in the boathouse.	☐	☐

▶ 7 4 B **Now listen to the first part of Chapter 5 and check your answers.**

Chapter 5

The Race

7 The following morning, Sam was at the boathouse very early. Mr Pullen was there. 'You're here early this Sunday morning,' he said. 'It's nice to see your brother back in the squad; perhaps he can be in the final eight! Come inside, it's raining. Cup of tea?'

'Yes, please!' said Sam, who didn't like tea.

Mr Pullen made the tea and Sam looked around the boathouse. *Where can I put Jason's recorder?* he thought.

'You can help me now you're here,' said Mr Pullen. 'I need to put that boat back in its place. He pointed to a yellow boat. 'We don't need it any more this year.'

Sam goes to the boathouse early. He helps Mr Pullen put a boat back in place and decides to hide the recorder behind the boat.

Sam went to help.

'You take that part. Yes, that's right. I can take this part, then we can carry it. Alright? One, two, three,' said Mr Pullen.

Together they carried the boat. And Sam saw the place. *Behind the boat!* That was a good place to put Jason's recorder. Mr Pullen went to get their tea, and Sam turned the recorder on and put it behind the yellow boat.

The Boat Race Mystery

'Here we are,' said Mr Pullen coming back from the kitchen, 'a nice cup of tea!'

'Thank you, Mr Pullen,' said Sam. 'It's half-term[1] next week. Can I come and help you sometimes?'

'Well, thank you, Sam. There are always a lot of jobs at the boathouse.'

8 On Monday, Sam went down to the river with Lisa. They helped clean the wheels on a seat and when Mr Pullen went to make some tea, Sam got the recorder and put it in his jacket. 'I don't like tea,' said Sam.

'Shh! Drink it! Then we can take this back to Jason,' said Lisa.

Back at Lisa's house, they ran up to Jason's room. 'Sorry, my computer's very slow,' he said.

Lisa and Sam watched the computer. There wasn't anything, only a long black line[2]. Then, they saw it; the line jumped for a second. Then they saw the long black line again.

'What was that noise?' said Jason, playing the recording again. 'I think that was a bird. Wait a minute, I can make it faster.'

There was nothing, only the long back line.

Lisa and Sam go back to the boathouse and get the recorder. Then they take it to Jason to listen to it on his computer, but there's nothing on the recorder.

[1] **half-term** half-term is a short school holiday. It's usually about a week

[2] **a line** this is a line ________ . You write on lines in an exercise book

'We can take the recorder back to the boathouse tomorrow,' said Sam, 'Lucky me, more tea!'

Two days later, Sam and Lisa were back in Jason's room. This time there was only the long black line, no bird and no person. 'We can put the recorder back in the boathouse tomorrow!' said Lisa, sadly.

The third time, they were lucky. After about twelve hours of recording, the long black line began to jump and jump. 'We've got something!' shouted Jason, pointing at the computer.

'What time was that?' said Sam.

'Nine o'clock last night,' said Lisa.

They put the recorder back in the boathouse and the third time they're lucky. This time they hear somebody walking in the boathouse, then someone talking about Max's seat in the boat, then a noise. It's sabotage again.

Jason stopped the recording. Then he put it back to a short time before the black line jumped. They listened. There it was! A door opened and they heard someone walking in the boathouse. The person walked around. Then it was quiet.

'Perhaps he's thinking,' said Sam.

'Shh,' said Jason.

They heard the person walking again. The next thing they heard was a voice! 'Eight, seven, six, five. Five, that's Max's seat!'

Then they heard a noise. 'Sabotage, again!' said Jason.

'Yes,' said Sam quietly. 'Shh.'

They heard some more noises, then a laugh. Then they heard the person walking again, the door closed and then nothing.

'That doesn't help us much,' said Lisa.

'Yes, it does,' answered Sam. 'You see, I know that voice. That's Shorty's *best friend!* That's *Pete Arnold!*

Sam knows the voice on the recorder. It's Pete Arnold's voice, Shorty's best friend!

• • •

It was a month later, and Sam, Lisa and Jason were in London, in a boat on the River Thames, following the Boat Race. Following the race from the river was very exciting. The crew wanted it and the coach wanted it. They wanted to say thank you to Sam, Lisa and Jason; thank you for stopping the sabotage. Now, in front of them, were the two crews: Oxford wearing dark blue and Cambridge wearing light blue. There were hundreds, no, *thousands* of people by the river and on the bridges, all watching the race on this cold, but sunny afternoon.

'Come on, Oxford!' shouted Lisa and Jason, jumping up and down in the boat. 'You can do it!'

Sam laughed as he watched his brother, the tallest man in the crew. 'Come on, Shorty!' he shouted. 'Come on, Oxford! PUSH!'

A month later Sam, Lisa and Jason are watching the Boat Race between Oxford and Cambridge from a boat on the River Thames in London. The crew and the coach want them to be there to say thank you for stopping the sabotage. Shorty is in the Oxford crew, too.

The race was very close, but Sam wasn't afraid. He looked at the thousands of people watching the race and he thought about Pete and Shorty's final conversation, before Pete followed the police to their car.

Pete did all the bad things because he wanted to row for Oxford like his father.

'Why did you do it, Pete?'

'I'm sorry. I'm not proud of myself. I wanted to row for Oxford, like my father.'

'But you were my friend. What about the ill rowers? You did a very bad thing. And poor Sid; he's hurt and he couldn't row in the Boat Race, because of you.'

Sam thought about his brother's words as he watched the two crews going around the final corner.

'We're in front!' shouted Lisa.

'We're winning!' shouted Jason.

Oxford wins the race and the coach says it's thanks to Sam, Lisa and Jason.

'Yes! We won!' shouted Sam, crying, as Oxford crossed the finish line in front of Cambridge.

'We did it! We did it, Coach! We won!' shouted Shorty from the boat.

'Yes, we won! But,' the coach pointed at Sam, Lisa and Jason, 'it was thanks to these three!'

Think

Were you surprised about Pete? Why? / Why not?

Sam, Lisa and Jason watch the Boat Race from a boat on the River Thames. Oxford wins!

OXFORD
BNY MELLON
BNY MELLON
BNY MELLON

Test your skills

21st Century Skills

1 ***The Boat Race Mystery* Physics Questions. Use the formulae for speed, distance and time to work out the answers.**

- speed (km per hour and metres per second) = distance/time. $s = d/t$
- distance (km) = speed x time. $d = s \times t$
- time (hours) = distance/speed. $t = d/s$

SPEED

1 Shorty runs 5 km in 0.5 hours (= 30 minutes). How fast does he run in km per hour? __________

2 Sam's school is 0.6 km from his house. Sometimes he walks fast, sometimes he's slow. Today he takes 0.15 hours (= 9 minutes) to arrive home. How fast does he walk in km per hour? __________

DISTANCE

3 The rowers row at 22.6 km per hour for 0.3 hours (= 18 minutes). How long is the race in km? __________

4 Lisa's baseball travels at 22 m per second for 3 seconds. How far does it go in metres? __________

TIME

5 The coach rides for 10 km at 20 km per hour. Is his bike ride 5 minutes, 50 minutes or 30 minutes? __________

6 The fire engine travels 6 km at 80 km per hour. Does it arrive at the boathouse after 7.5 minutes, 4.5 minutes, or 75 minutes? __________

Reading and Writing MOVERS

2 Look at this picture from Chapter 5. Complete the sentences and answer the questions.

The rowers in the picture are in the Oxford *crew*.

1 Sam, Lisa and Jason are watching the race from a ________.

2 What colour is the Oxford boat? ________

3 What can you see behind the three friends? ________

4 Why are the rowers happy? ________

Writing and Speaking

21st Century Skills

3A Did you enjoy *The Boat Race Mystery*? Complete the sentences.

I liked / didn't like *The Boat Race Mystery*, because ________
________.

A character I liked was ________ because
________.

A character I didn't like was ________ because
________.

3B Reading Quiz. Work in pairs to answer the quiz.

ARE YOU A BOOKWORM?

1 How many books do you read every year?

- a ☐ none
- b ☐ two or three
- c ☐ more than ten
- d ☐ ________

2 What other things do you read?

- a ☐ blogs
- b ☐ magazines
- c ☐ newspapers
- d ☐ ________

3 Tick the type of books you like best.

- a ☐ thrillers & detective
- b ☐ adventure
- c ☐ love stories
- d ☐ historical drama
- e ☐ biographies
- f ☐ horror
- g ☐ science fiction
- h ☐ ________

4 What's your favourite book?

____

Focus on...

Oxford and Cambridge

Oxford and Cambridge are home to two of the oldest and most famous universities in the world. Oxford is the southern half of the UK and Cambridge is in the east.

The City of Cambridge

Cambridge has a population of about 129,000. It is in the east of the UK on the River Cam. Cambridge was famous for farming in the past, but today it is more famous for technology and education. There are a lot of computer and science companies in Cambridge. It is a very beautiful city and tourism is also important.

The City of Oxford

Oxford is larger than Cambridge and has a population of about 153,000. Oxford is on the River Thames and the city's name comes from *ox* (a large farm animal) and *ford* (a place without a bridge where you can cross a river). In the twentieth century, many Oxford people worked in car making, but today only the Mini is made there. Today, more people work in information technology, science and education. It is also an important tourist centre.

The University of Cambridge

The University of Cambridge (founded 1209) is one of the world's oldest universities, after Bologna (1088) and Oxford (1098). There are 31 colleges at the university and there are about 18,500 students and about 6,000 academic staff. Some students live in their college and others live in rooms in the town. The oldest college in Cambridge is Peterhouse (1284) and the newest is Robinson (1977).

The University of Oxford

Oxford is older than Cambridge and a little bigger; there are 38 colleges and about 24,000 students. It also has the largest university library in the UK, with more than 11 million books and papers. Most of the books are underground! The oldest colleges in Oxford are University, Balliol and Merton (thirteenth century). The newest college is Kellogg (1990).

Complete the table about Oxford and Cambridge.

	Cambridge	Oxford
Population		
Name of river		
Main industries		
Founded in	*1209*	
Number of colleges		
Number of students		
Oldest college(s)		

Focus on...

The Oxford and Cambridge Boat Race

Sport is very important at Oxford and Cambridge. When the two universities play against each other in a sport, people in the team usually get a Blue – this says that they are top sports people. Rowing, cricket and rugby are the most famous Oxford-Cambridge matches.

History

The first Oxford and Cambridge Boat Race was in 1829 and Oxford won. In 1856, the universities started having the race every year on the River Thames in London. The first women's Boat Race was in 1927, but they didn't have the race every year till the 1960s.

The Course

The Boat Race is on the River Thames in London and it goes from Putney Bridge to Mortlake, which is 4.2 miles or about 6.8 kilometres. The fastest race was in 1998, when Cambridge won in 16 minutes and 9 seconds.

The Boat Race Today

Today, the race is usually on the last Sunday in March or the first Sunday in April. It is an important race in Britain. Many people watch it on television and many others go to London to see the race. They watch from the side of the river and from the many bridges over the River Thames.

Boat Race Facts

The crews don't always finish the Boat Race. Sometimes the weather is so bad that a boat sinks (goes under the water). In 1984, Cambridge sank after an accident with another boat and in 1912, both Oxford and Cambridge sank!
At the end of the race, the cox (the person who steers the boat and co-ordinates the rowers) of the winning crew goes into the river – the crew throws him or her into the water.

Online research. What's the most famous sporting event in your country? Write some sentences about it.

Which sport is it? ______________________

When is it? ______________________

Where is it? ______________________

How many people watch it? ______________________

Test Yourself

How many words can you remember from the glossary? Use the clues to complete the crossword.

Clues Across

3 There are 2 of these on a bike. There are 4 on a car. (5 letters)

7 You ________ at school in the morning and you leave school in the afternoon. (6 letters)

9 When you have an accident and you do something bad to your body, you ________ your body. (4 letters)

10 When a room is dark, you need this to see. (5 letters)

12 Sam doesn't know what to do. He thinks for a minute, then he sends a message. (6 letters)

13 To go behind someone and go to the same places. (6 letters)

Clues Down

1 You make a lot of noise when you speak. (5 letters)

2 When you say, 'First I'll do this, then I'll do this, then I'll do this,' you're making a ________ . (4 letters)

4 People do this when they are sad. (3 letters)

5 You sit on this in a boat. (4 letters)

6 You make this noise because you are happy. (5 letters)

8 You open your mouth and use this when you speak. (5 letters)

11 When you stop riding your bike, you ________ (3+3 letters)

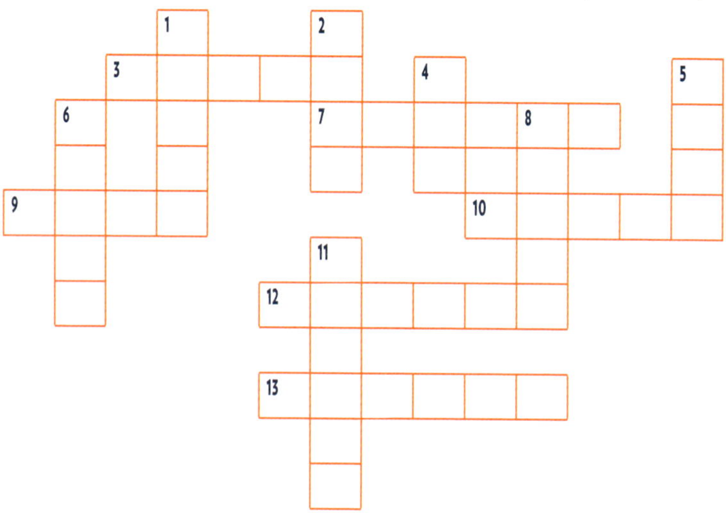

Syllabus

Articles
A, an, the

Nouns
Singular and plural forms, common irregular plural forms, countable and uncountable, possessive *'s*

Pronouns
Personal, subject, direct object, indirect object, demonstrative *this, that, it + be* in impersonal expressions

Adjectives
Simple adjectives (attributive and predicative), possessive adjectives, comparative and superlative adjectives

Adverbs
Frequency, manner

Prepositions
Place, time, movement

Conjunctions
And, but, or, because

Quantifiers
Some, any

Verbs
Present simple, present continuous, future with present continuous, *going to* and *will*, past simple regular and irregular forms, imperative, verb + infinitive, verb + *-ing*, infinitive of purpose, *want someone to do something, must/mustn't, have to/had to, would* and *wouldn't like, need*

Topics
Sport, friendship, teams, problem-solving

Teen ELi Readers

Stage 1

Maureen Simpson, *In Search of a Missing Friend*
Charles Dickens, *Oliver Twist*
Geoffrey Chaucer, *The Canterbury Tales*
Janet Borsbey & Ruth Swan, *The Boat Race Mystery*
Lucy Maud Montgomery, *Anne of Green Gables*
Mark Twain, *A Connecticut Yankee in King Arthur's Court*
Mark Twain, *The Adventures of Huckleberry Finn*
Angela Tomkinson, *Great Friends!*
Edith Nesbit, *The Railway Children*
Eleanor H. Porter, *Pollyanna*
Anna Sewell, *Black Beauty*
Kenneth Grahame, *The Wind in the Willows*

Stage 2

Elizabeth Ferretti, *Dear Diary...*
Angela Tomkinson, *Loving London*
Mark Twain, *The Adventures of Tom Sawyer*
Mary Flagan, *The Egyptian Souvenir*
Maria Luisa Banfi, *A Faraway World*
Frances Hodgson Burnett, *The Secret Garden*
Robert Louis Stevenson, *Treasure Island*
Elizabeth Ferretti, *Adventure at Haydon Point*
William Shakespeare, *The Tempest*
Angela Tomkinson, *Enjoy New York*
Frances Hodgson Burnett, *Little Lord Fauntleroy*
Michael Lacey Freeman, *Egghead*
Michael Lacey Freeman, *Dot to Dot*
Silvana Sardi, *The Boy with the Red Balloon*
Silvana Sardi, *Scotland is Magic!*
Silvana Sardi, *Garpur: My Iceland*
Silvana Sardi, *Follow your Dreams*
Gabriele Rebagliati, *Naoko: My Japan*

Stage 3

Anna Claudia Ramos, *Expedition Brazil*
Charles Dickens, *David Copperfield*
Mary Flagan, *Val's Diary*
Maureen Simpson, *Destination Karminia*
Anonymous, *Robin Hood*
Jack London, *The Call of the Wild*
Louisa May Alcott, *Little Women*
Gordon Gamlin, *Allan: My Vancouver*